Esther in Exile

Esther in Exile

Toward a Spirituality of Difference

CHRISTIANNE MÉROZ

TRANSLATED BY DENNIS WIENK

WIPF & STOCK · Eugene, Oregon

Contents

Preface

"More than a woman alone in the world,
  An exile."

Le Carnet des nuits, Marie Laurencin[1]

My goal is not simply to present the mysterious and marvelous adventure of Esther and the Jewish deportees to Mesopotamia. The book of Esther confronts us with questions which are very much alive today: the absence of God, violence, racism, anti-Semitism, the condition of women, immigration.

This narrative bears powerful witness to the Jewish experience of exile, an exile that is both spiritual and geographical. In this special and unique story we discover a dimension of the human experience and faithful living present in every century, alongside our own condition as nomads, strangers, and travelers on earth. This text truly belongs to the heritage of the whole human race.

This journey to the end of exile, as it unveils its many faces to us, meets us in our personal stories, in our own exiles. In situations of radical upheaval it shows how important it is to remain faithful to one's identity. Between the ghetto and assimilation there is often no other solution than that of disobedience in the name of an

---

1. Laurencin, *Le Carnet des nuits*, 63.

existential obedience, the obedience one owes to that God who is hidden at the core of being, to that God who is hidden at the very heart of history.

I am profoundly convinced that today only the messages that come through an authentic human experience can communicate something essential to us. That is why I believe that the book of Esther deserves to be discovered, or rediscovered, by all those women and men who like Esther and Mordecai are also tirelessly searching for God.

What a beautiful lesson in spirituality we find here! We do not meet a woman or a man at ease with themselves, managing their anguish the way one manages one's stock portfolio. This is not a story of brightness that banishes the darkness of the world. It is rather a lesson of gentle strength that bears with the darkness right to the end.

Christianne Méroz

Introduction

A Subversive Book

THE STORY OF ESTHER takes place in the Persian Empire at Susa, one of its three capitals, at the time of King Ahasuerus, whom we identify as either Xerxes I (486–465 BCE) or Artaxerxes (465–424). Before discussing the principal themes of the story it is worthwhile to recall the thread of events.

A STORY OF FEASTS

In the third year of his reign after six months of feasting, Ahasuerus offers a banquet of seven days to the men of his kingdom while his wife Vashti entertains the women. On the last day of the festival, the king is intoxicated and demands that the queen come and expose her beauty before all the guests. She refuses to participate in such an exhibition. Ahasuerus, fearing lest his wife's disobedience incite the other women to behave similarly, divorces her by an irrevocable decree.

In order to replace the deposed queen, a search is then begun for a new wife, a "better wife" than Vashti. Among the girls brought to the royal harem is a young Jewish orphan, exiled to Persia with her uncle Mordecai who serves as her tutor. It is Esther. Ahasuerus is seduced by her great beauty and chooses her to succeed Vashti.

So it is that a young Jewish woman becomes queen of Persia. However, on the advice of her uncle, she does not reveal her full identity.

During this time Mordecai learns of a plot against the king. He tells Esther, who in turn informs the king. And the fact is inscribed according to custom in the book of the royal annals.

A new character appears on stage, Haman the head official of the realm. Conscious of his importance, Haman demands that all bow down before him. Mordecai, for whom this gesture of submission is reserved for God alone, refuses. Exasperated, Haman decides to finish him off, and with him all his coreligionists. He obtains from the king an irrevocable decree condemning all the Jews to extermination, scheduled by lot for the thirteenth day of the month of Adar (sometime in February or March).

Weeping and lamentation arose immediately from the Jewish population. And Mordecai begged Esther to convince the king to lift the decree. But Esther knew that it was a rule that no one, not even herself, could enter the king's presence without having been called. Therefore she decides to fast for three days and three nights first, after which, just perhaps, the king will consent to receive her. This is in fact what happens. However, she does not speak of the object of her visit right away. As she planned to do, she simply invites him to a banquet, along with Haman. Haman does not sense the trap, but believes that he has arrived at the summit of his glory and thinks that now is the time to execute Mordecai.

While Haman is in the process of having the gallows erected, Ahasuerus, who suffered from insomnia, asks that someone read the annals to him. There he discovers that Mordecai, who had saved him from treachery, has not been compensated. At this very moment, Haman enters his presence to ask for Mordecai's death. He doesn't have time to open his mouth before the king asks him what he thinks appropriate to do in order to honor someone whose conduct was exemplary. Not doubting for an instant that it was all about himself, Haman proposes the greatest honors to the king. Of course he is dumbfounded to learn that it was really all about Mordecai. The only thing he can do is obey the king's order.

In the course of another banquet given by Esther for the king and his head official, she reveals her Jewish identity and denounces the threat of extermination which Haman's hatred is causing to hang over her people and herself. Very troubled by these revelations, Ahasuerus retires into his garden and, at the moment when he returns to the banquet hall, he catches Haman bending over the queen's chair begging her to intervene in his favor. Thinking that his official is going to violate his wife, the king gives an immediate order that he be hung on the gallows which Haman had himself prepared for Mordecai.

Mordecai therefore takes Haman's place, and the king agrees to promulgate a new decree authorizing the Jews to defend themselves at the time of the massacre scheduled for 13 Adar. Thus, thanks to the support of the king, the Jews can exercise their lawful right of self-defense. On the evening of 14 Adar, eight hundred dead are counted among the ranks of Persian anti-Semites.

To commemorate this victory and thank God for having reversed the course of history, Esther and Mordecai institute a day of thanksgiving on the 14 Adar. This will be the feast of Purim, or Lots, in commemoration of the drawing of lots by which Haman had set the date for the extermination of the Jews.

IN ORDER TO RELIVE THE STORY

In the Hebrew Bible the book of Esther is the last of the Five Scrolls—Song of Songs, Ruth, Lamentations, Ecclesiastes, Esther. The Hebrew word for scroll is *megillah*, and this is the name the Jews have chosen for the book of Esther. It is read last in the synagogue service. On the feast of Purim it is read twice, at the prayers after sundown and the next day at morning prayers.

Children learn this simple, dramatic, fascinating story early on. This is perhaps one of the reasons for its popularity, along with the custom of having a Megillah on richly illuminated parchment in the home.

On the feast of Purim, the reading of the scroll of Esther in the synagogue is the occasion of a theatrical skit, a sort of psychodrama. Children, and sometimes the adults too, dress up. Certain verses are recited very loudly by the whole congregation (Esth 2:5; 8:15–16; 10:3)—regrettably only the verses concerning Mordecai, thus leaving the decisive role played by Esther in the shadows. When evil Haman's name is said, the children shake rattles or stomp their feet because this character in the story has become the prototype of all the executioners of the Jews, and his fall from grace has been a source of hope and refuge in the face of suffering and persecutions across the centuries.

The book of Esther illustrates the everlasting miracle of the survival of the Jewish people. In the midst of the Nazi oppression Edith Stein drew courage from it. She wrote, "I am a little Esther, very poor and very weak, but the king who has chosen me is much greater and infinitely merciful."

However, Purim is not simply a joyous carnival time. All are asked to remember their neighbors and give presents to their friends and gifts of money or in kind to the poor. For joy cannot be complete without acts of sharing and solidarity.

SOMETHING DISTURBING

The book of Esther is a bewildering and disturbing book. In spite of numerous contradictions and confusions which mark the story, the author situates the plot after the second wave of deportations of the Jews. Xerxes I was reigning in Persia at that time. With the exception of a small minority who will profit from the edict of Cyrus in 538 and return to Judah, a majority of the Jews settled down in Persia, many of them even enjoying relatively important positions in political and economic matters.

How does it happen then, taking into account this favorable situation, that the author of the book of Esther insists so on Haman's anti-Semitic hatred and on the telling of a story that would include the terrible massacre of the Jewish population?

The book was of course redacted much later, very probably at the beginning of the second century BCE, during the reign of Antiochus IV, Antiochus Epiphanes. In his vast empire, from Greece to India, he had forbidden Jews from practicing their religion, going even as far as to dedicate the Jerusalem temple to Olympian Zeus. So it is to encourage fellow Jews under persecution not to give way to despair that an anonymous author redacted this book. At whatever time it was written, it is evident that it recounts a traditional story going back to the Persian period. Having admitted the mixed origins of the work, we suggest for our purposes that we ponder the message of this first biblical novel and try to ferret out its import for the time.

At the level of the story and its interpretation the book of Esther has raised great controversies, which rendered its inclusion in the Bible problematic. Many have suggested that the absence of the word "God" would be a good enough reason to have excluded it, and the hostility that it exhibits toward other nations is usually instanced as well.

We should not be surprised then to learn that readers sought to spiritualize it early on. The Greek translation, the Septuagint which was made in Egypt where there was an important Jewish community, is a clear sign of this tendency. That translation is in fact interesting in this respect, that it introduces a number of additions into the Hebrew text—prayers and especially the explicit mention of God at key moments in the story.

THE CHARACTERS ARE SYMBOLIC

With the exception of Ahasuerus none of the characters in the book of Esther is known to history. The good reason for this is that it is a novel, which reflects the customs and situations of the author's own time, namely, the second century. The characters are therefore symbolic.

Ahasuarus is the portrait of a foreign king. His arbitrary power allows him by divine right to promulgate irrevocable decrees, of the kind that can only arouse from the Jewish minority the same kind of violence that he uses for his own purpose.

As for Vashti, the valiant queen Vashti, her name appears nowhere else than here. The tradition that sees her as the granddaughter of Nebuchadnezzar casts her from the outset among the enemies of the Jews.

Haman, the chief official, is a descendant of the king of the Amalekites (Esth 3:1). In this way the author presents him to us as evil incarnate. In fact at the time of Amalek's battle with Agag, victorious Saul let him go with his life and thus disobeyed God. In showing himself more merciful than the God of mercy, he allowed evil to pursue its course (1 Sam 15:8–9). This is why, according to tradition, Haman, the sworn enemy of the Jews in exile, is portrayed as a descendant of Agag (cf. Exod 17:8–16; Num 24:7–20; Deut 25:17–19; 1 Sam 15:2–3).

It is therefore not by chance that the story tells us that Mordecai and Esther both descend from king Saul (Esth 2:5–6), since their role will be to redeem the sin of their ancestor in trying to eradicate the destructive hatred that dogs the Jewish people. Seen from this angle, the book of Esther teaches us about the need to fight against evil in order that it not continue from generation to generation.

On the other hand, when we consider the book through the symbolism of the names of its two heroes, it appears as a resistance piece. Indeed, Esther and Mordecai's names derive from those of the two gods, Ishtar and Marduk, who played a central role in the great Babylonian New Year festival from the beginning of time.

So the book of Esther culminates in the festival of Purim, the commemoration of the salvation of the Jews, a reversal that substituted their deliverance for the threat of their extermination. This festival has a very special character since it is not, like the other holidays, prescribed in the Torah. Purim was probably therefore an "anti-festival" for the Jews in exile to celebrate in the spring in place of the Babylonian festival. Its solemn institution by Mordecai and Esther (Esth 9:20–23) may have provided a new way of being a Jew in exile. The book of Esther thus shows that it is possible to integrate into an alien society without assimilating entirely, without losing or denying one's roots. From this perspective the Megillah takes its place in the genre of subversive literature.

A DRAMATIC DESTINY

It is not surprising that the great French poet and playwright Jean Racine made Esther the hero of one of his tragedies. The most dramatic feature of her story is the destiny of this woman, which is marked from beginning to end by her status as an exile.

Her accession to royalty will not fundamentally change her situation. Even after becoming queen of Persia, she will not stop being one of these thousands of Jews who live in captivity, in the diaspora far from their country. Furthermore, as a woman she is familiar with that particular form of exile that consists of living in a patriarchal society where she is considered as an object, the property of a man, and not as a subject, a person in her own right. She experiences that harsh reality in the harem where, an exile in exile, she must submit for a year to customs entirely foreign to those of her people. Twelve months of caring for her looks so that she can respond to the tastes and desires of the king whenever he wants her. Twelve months of being sidelined in order to be sure that she is not pregnant or carrying a disease. In short, twelve months of humiliation for this woman whom one strand of Jewish tradition presents not as Mordecai's niece or cousin—literally Esther 2:7 says that she is "the daughter of her uncle"—but as Mordecai's wife.

Niece or cousin or wife or daughter—on this score doubt is possible. The text reads thus: "when her father and her mother died, Mordecai adopted her as his own daughter." The Hebrew word can be taken either as "daughter" or "house," since the consonants of these two words are the same, the vowels not being written. This is why Jewish commentators suggest we read that Mordecai had not taken her "as his own daughter" but "as his own house," that is, as a wife, the one who keeps house for her husband. The Greek translators understood that Mordecai had adopted Esther "with the intention of making her his wife," without making it clear if he had already done so at the time of the story.

These readings of the text are not exclusive. We are free to choose and have chosen to see Esther as Mordecai's spouse, not his cousin or niece or daughter.

THE BLACK AND THE WHITE OF TORAH

Besides, it is one of the gifts of Jewish tradition that, when confronted with silence in the biblical texts, we read what is called
"the black and the white of Torah," that is, the written words (the
black) and what is not explicitly written in the text but ought to be
taken into account, what is not said (the white). So Torah is made
up of the white as much as it is of the black, and the white of Torah
is constantly offering us space for contemplation by what it doesn't
say, by its silences.

These open places, these opportunities for meditation, can
be filled by passages, words, expressions where allusion has been
made to a reality, a behavior, an event, or a meaning without any
clear specificity. These are blanks that can be filled in to the extent
of the reader's knowledge, experience, and creativity.

However, in reading the Bible, this freedom does have its limits. The framework of tradition should be respected, as well as the
rule that the Bible itself is its own best commentary.

To take an example, in Luke's gospel we read, "His mother
treasured all these things in her heart" (Luke 2:51). What are "all
these things?" In the context we can certainly fill in this blank with
what comes before: the angel Gabriel's words at the time of the
Annunciation, the Visitation, the appearance of the angel to the
shepherds, even the birth of Jesus. But we can also fill it with texts
borrowed from the Hebrew Bible: the song of Hannah, the mother
of Samuel (1 Sam 2:1–10); verses from the Psalms (87; 139); verses
from Proverbs (Prov 31:10–31). We also have recourse to our own
experience of being a parent, recalling the anguish we suffer over
some of our children's choices and the moods that follow.

In the case of Mary herself we can imagine that her mind
might have been tormented by her status as an unwed mother,
by all the questions that must have flooded her mind concerning
the birth and upbringing of such a special son. Perhaps she is also
remembering that woman whose name she bears, Miriam, who
had made it possible for Moses, all those centuries before, to escape death and become the Savior of Israel (cf. Exod 2:4; Mic 6:4).

Would Mary the mother of Jesus also have a messianic vocation? "All these things" have been considered by numerous male commentators. Is it not also important that women be heard from?

Such a blank page, an open place, a white space invites creativity, personalized reading, bringing to life, an "infinite reading," as some call it. Certainly what we have here is one of the most fertile resources of our tradition. For us women these open places offer space where we can slip into the tradition in order to enrich it with commentaries and interpretations that reflect our way of reading the text as we insert our own experience as women. This way of making the female voice heard is part and parcel of the living tradition of Judaism, that of midrashic interpretation as it is called. A midrash is a text, sometimes a story, which serves as a commentary on a biblical passage.

SPACES FOR MEDITATION

In this regard it is striking to note that the Greek version, the Septuagint, whose additions to the Hebrew text we noted above, functions in just this way. Indeed, the passages marked in that version with the letters A, B, C, D, E, and F are really interpretations of verses in the Hebrew text that were open to certain questions.

Thus Addition A, Mordecai's dream, refers to Mordecai's recommendation to Esther to say nothing about her origin (2:10). It lets us foresee that Esther is most assuredly called to play an important role in the liberation of the exiles when they are faced with the threat of death. Additions B and E make explicit one of the decrees of extermination (3:12), and the letter for the vindication of the Jews (8:11–14). Addition C gives the content of Mordecai's and Esther's prayers and shows us important aspects of their faith, the deep source of their actions. And Addition D shows us what the meeting between Esther and Ahasuerus could look like after the queen's three days of fasting and prayer (5:1–2).

These passages in the Greek translation are both commentaries and interpretations and offer a certain spirituality to the book, a way of permitting us to see, at the heart of the story, the action of a God so hidden as to seem absent. In this way Addition F, artfully placed at the end of the text, gives us the interpretation of Mordecai's dream, which opens the story and provides the key to understanding the whole book.

This rereading of the Hebrew text by the Greek version presents us with the events of the Megillah not as a series of chance happenings, but as a coherent process, a divine plan. God has not abandoned the people. At the heart of exile, God is present and acting. What Mordecai's dream could only suggest is ultimately revealed to be the case.

Trying to make the older text (Hebrew) and the revised text (Greek) talk to each other can perhaps help us more easily understand that the joy that breaks out at the end of the book is more the expression of an immense act of thanksgiving to God than a song of triumph. Of course this rereading does not alleviate the bitter taste that remains when we find ourselves having to affirm in the end that only violence seems to succeed in suppressing evil and not the force of good and forgiveness.

ESTHER, OUR SISTER

As a work of fiction full of symbolism, the book of Esther lends itself particularly well to a many-voiced reading. Using the story's various themes, we will engage in successive readings, letting Jewish exegesis inspire us when it suggests fresh perspectives. The guiding thread that will supply unity to our commentary, which will take a circular rather than linear or "logical" form, is the theme of exile and the consequences which ensue.

What seems to be the most dramatic feature of the story is this destiny that is marked out from beginning to end by the tragedy of exile, or better yet by interlocking exiles, after the pattern of nesting figurines. Thus Esther is not only exiled in the sense of being a deportee from her homeland; but successively exiled from her own people, from her family; and in the harem and then on the throne, exiled in the solitude of those people in high places who wield power.

First it is a geographic exile, then an interior, more spiritual than psychological, exile. Exile is the multifaceted reality that goes right through her life as a woman, a wife, and a Jew, and in unique fashion seals all the aspects of her existence. A symbolic figure, archetype of all kinds of exiles, Esther, harrowed by that harsh reality, becomes a sister, a friend, a companion for our time. As an icon of exile, the Megillah demonstrates a surprising topicality.

1

Exile: Challenge and Opportunity

AFTER THE FALL OF the temple and the second wave of deportations, a profound change took place in the outlook of the Judeans. We have the first signs of it in the message of the prophet Jeremiah who had announced this upheaval, and the experience of exile will be the crucible of this transformation. At this juncture in their history the Jews feel that they are in the midst of both a personal and a national reassessment of what their future will bring.

A TIME OF CHANGE

The dispersion is no longer just a speculation; it has become a terrible reality. And the destruction of the temple in 587 BCE produces such a shock that Judean society is transformed into Jewish society, to the extent that, as has often been observed, Jeremiah could be said to be one of the last Judeans and one of the first Jews. We are present at the emergence of a new way of being faithful. As never before, the faith is being expressed in a very personal way. Jeremiah started it all when he showed that the return to God necessarily involves a return to one's self, through a search for personal unity. The prophet does not hesitate to speak of his doubts, of his anxiety, of his inner struggles, of his rebellion. By personal prayer, lamentation, and intimate conversations with God, the relationship between the human and the divine becomes individualized.

The prayers of Mordecai and Esther are excellent examples of this (Add EsthC). Even though they both believe in the justice and mercy of God, the threat of extermination hanging over the Jews revolts them and touches them so deeply that they have no doubt but that God suffers along with them.

The proximity of an apparently silent God does not prevent Esther from bewailing her suffering in words that rightly reflect her distress as a woman. She even goes so far as to compare her royal crown with a sanitary napkin, so much does her role disgust her (Add EsthC 14:16).

In exile and without the temple, the rites that before were at the heart of daily life are no longer possible. To remain faithful to oneself and to God, one has to turn to more interiorized religious practices, more personal and more hidden practices. Thus transition from the visible to the invisible comes about. New fundamental themes emerge, onto which centuries later, to extend Paul's metaphor in Romans 11, the teaching of Jesus will be grafted. Circumcision will be not only of the flesh but of the heart, worship of God not only in a particular place but in spirit and in truth.

Heartfelt adherence is henceforth more explicitly part of the external rites, which do not become any less important. Traditional living is supplemented with soul; spirituality enlivens matters of the law. And by means of a constant dialogue between the external acts of life and the interior life, between collective and individual history, a profound and needed change is born in the very heart of exile.

HOW TO REMAIN FAITHFUL

For Esther and Mordecai, as members of the Jewish community in Susa, the basic question is this—how to continue living with God when there is no more temple, or land, or holy city, when all that gathered and grounded their hope suddenly goes missing? Is

God's project for creation still practical when they find themselves dispersed throughout the 127 provinces of the Persian Empire, from India to Ethiopia?

The book of Esther does not necessarily respond affirmatively to this question. It affirms the possibility of being morally and spiritually faithful to Torah without the temple and far from the holy land. But to effect this transition, an urgent task demands attention, namely, to give a different look to the realization of God's plan. Instead of participating in a common project, that of a people, each exile must from now on look for how to realize it individually, wherever they find themselves and under their own conditions. So it is that Mordecai and Esther will discover bit by bit first an individual and then collective meaning that will make sense of their adventure.

Exile certainly remains a trial and a suffering, but how they view it as they take it on makes it a kind of learning process. It becomes a divinely pedagogic time. This is not however to reduce exile to a mere learning experience, which would be cynical at the very least, but rather to discern how women and men have arrived, during a time of crisis and upheaval, at renewing their relationship with God and adapting and integrating themselves into a different cultural context without losing their identity, without finding themselves uprooted.

What will allow the exiles to preserve individual and community unity is to sink their roots no longer into a land but into the very Word of God, now engraved on the heart. What formerly bound them to God and consequently to each other they discover is no longer the temple but the bond of love, a bond that knows no limit, no boundary. Did not the divine presence—a feminine noun in Hebrew—also leave for exile with the deportees (Ezek 10:18–19; 11:22–23)? So wherever a human being is, she or he must be able to find God. This quest, however, necessarily gives way to interiorization and individualization of piety as each woman and each man becomes the dwelling place for God.

INTEGRATING WITHOUT BECOMING LOST

From now on it is very important that men and women who know how to read the signs of the times and who dare prophetic words and acts rise up in the midst of social disarray. Esther and Mordecai are among those who search tirelessly for the meaning of history and evidence of God's presence in the confusion of exile. Faithfulness and memory are essential for such a project. They allow history to be transformed with new births, and they keep essential values from being clouded over in the storm of exile.

The prophet Ezekiel reminds us that this attitude of wakefulness and vigilance was not much in evidence at that time. In fact a large number of Judeans had chosen to assimilate. Material life was relatively easy because Babylonian culture was rich and refined. In parallel fashion despair and fear had pushed more than one exile to melt into the masses in order to seek anonymity. Ezekiel calls them all dry bones (Ezek 37:11).

But others became resisters, who were going to make sure there would be continuity amidst the change. These people certainly also had to adapt, and, as the story of Esther shows us, they did. There is however a threshold that they refused to cross, the threshold of assimilation which would have meant denying their origins, their roots, and still more their part in a divine project which, if it seemed to pass them by for the moment, had not, for all that, become null and void. So they refused to be among Ezekiel's living dead.

With faithfulness to the depths of their identity, Esther and Mordecai will succeed in turning the path of exile, apparently a pathway with no outlet, into a paschal path, a pathway of knowledge. Having left their country involuntarily, they will proceed voluntarily to rediscover themselves. This often dark and laborious project will appear as a positive step in the end. They will discover in the chaos of exile, in the apparent absence of God, that it is not a path of annihilation, but on the contrary that it leads to new self-knowledge, as well as to new knowledge of God, of the one who puts breath in all people so that they may truly live (Ezek 37:5, 14).

2

Memorable Banquets

IN THE HEBREW BIBLE the word for "banquet" occurs forty-six times, of which twenty are in the book of Esther. That certainly shows how important the role of banquets is in the story. We can count seven banquets altogether, and as in a symphony we can divide them into three movements.

The first movement consists of the fabulous banquet Ahasuerus gave in honor of the nobility, lasting 180 days (Esth 1:3–4), which is followed by a banquet of seven days for the people (1:5), and Vashti's banquet for the women (1:9). These banquets celebrate the triumph of godlessness over the divine prophecies. They are the expression of contempt of the Persian conquerors toward God and the exiles. We remember that it is during these banquets that Vashti will lose her place on the throne and that Esther, after a time of probation, will be crowned queen in the course of yet another banquet (2:18).

The second movement opens on the first of two banquets that Esther, after her fast, offers to the king and to Haman the head official (5:3–5, 8; 7:1). It is during the second banquet of this movement that we are present at Haman's fall and that Esther obtains the liberation of the Jews. These two feasts, as we will see, are accompanied by supplications to God. The moment for a divine intervention has finally arrived.

The third movement is the banquet of joy at the end of the book. It celebrates the thanksgiving of the Jews to God for the great reversal of history (9:17).

These are three movements, three kinds of banquets, each with its special coloration.

THE WEIGHT OF A PROPHECY

Ahasuerus and Vashti's banquets are expressions of great relief. In an ironic fashion they are signs of the non-accomplishment of the divine prophecies. For a century the prophecies of Jeremiah had haunted the monarchs. They proclaimed that when seventy years had run their course for Babylon, God would fulfill the promise to return the exiles to their country, which would effectively signal the ruin of their oppressors (Jer 25:11–14; 29:10). So while the prophecy remained unsettled, kings avoided committing acts that would provoke the divine anger. They lived in fear and hope at the same time that the destruction of the Jerusalem temple had put an end to the ascendancy of the God of the Judeans.

Seventy years was a quasi-magical number for kings who one after the other applied themselves to counting them. Having counted seventy years from Nebuchadnezzar's accession, Balthazar was the first to believe that the time had run out. He rejoiced in it and prepared an orgiastic banquet, legendary in the literature of extravagance. On this occasion he dared God by using the sacred vessels from the temple. He paid for this folly with his life, for he was assassinated the same night. Cyrus remained comparatively more prudent during his reign.

When Ahasuerus mounted the throne, like his predecessors he too had his eyes fixed on the calendar. According to his calculations, the seventy years should come to an end with the third year of his reign. Having arrived at the long-expected day, he celebrates with the famous banquet of 180 days with which the book of Esther opens. He in turn does not hesitate to serve the wine in the sacred vessels of the temple (1:7). Deeply saddened by this profanation, certain Jews present at the banquet, among them Mordecai, decided to leave the feast. However, Ahasuerus was not punished directly for this act because God needed him in order to intervene in the course of history by means of his future queen.

AT ESTHER'S TABLE

Nine years have passed (3:7), and Esther is reigning alongside Ahasuerus. Haman, the chief official, enjoys a privileged position. As we know, all subjects had to bow before him. But Mordecai, for whom such an act is reserved for God, refuses and thus provokes the anger of the great man who decides to have all the Jews exterminated. This is the context of Esther's two banquets. If Ahasuerus's feasts had been a way of mocking God and God's prophets, those of his wife will take the form of prayers to God. They will also be the occasion of Haman's fall.

So after three days and three nights of fasting, Esther appears before the king who in the course of the two banquets asks her three times what she desires (5:3, 6; 7:2). The first time she answers: "If it pleases the king, let the king and Haman come today to a banquet that I have prepared for the king" (5:4). How different is Esther's answer from that of Vashti! But in both instances we are in the presence of women who effect change.

The attitude of Vashti, who refuses categorically to respond to Ahasuerus's wish that she exhibit her beauty, shows the spontaneity of a woman wounded by the demands of a tyrannical husband. What woman would not be outraged to learn that her husband desires that she expose herself in front of his guests? In refusing to undress in front of drunken men, Vashti chooses to behave in a way that firmly underscores her dignity. She does not submit, and we know that this liberty she takes is going to occasion her downfall and disappearance, but not without profoundly destabilizing the patriarchal system (1:16–18).

Esther for her part chooses an entirely different way of acting. On the outside she appears submissive, but she nonetheless sticks to her design, a secret plan. She wants, if possible, to save her people from Haman's anti-Semitic claws. Her tactic is composed at once of charm and address, of finesse and intelligence.

We have examples of it in her responses to Ahasuerus. However, pressed to say what has brought her into the king's presence, Esther remains silent and pretends that she has come to invite him to a banquet. This is a good way to surprise, for there is no risk to life in coming in person before the king just to deliver an invitation! In acting this way, Esther is certainly complying with the customs of the court where she knows how much feasts are appreciated, but she is especially anxious to have the encounter seen as a convivial opportunity, just for the pleasure of being together. She preserves friendly relations and puts her request in a light that is entirely characteristic. Canceling the decree for the extermination of the Jewish population—or more exactly because a royal order could not be cancelled (8:8), and the promulgation of another decree recognizing their right of legitimate defense is required—is not a small affair that can be settled in so many words. It is a very concrete matter of saving human lives.

So Esther takes the necessary time and applies all her charm. Let us not doubt that she will act when the right moment comes. Meanwhile she shows formidable cunning by inviting Haman himself to join the feast. During that time he will be cleverly neutralized and not able to carry out his plot, and, once the plot is uncovered, not able to organize a defense. Furthermore, although the presence of the chief official could arouse the king's jealousy, it will also allow Ahasuerus to eliminate him as a potential rival. We see that Esther's strategy had been meticulously planned.

THE PRESENCE OF A HIDDEN GOD

According to the sages of the Talmud, that immense collection of commentaries on the Torah (around 500 CE), the text of the book of Esther teaches us even more about the intelligence and integrity of its central figure. For example, while God is not mentioned by name, the word "king" on the other hand appears more than two hundred fifty times. The commentaries claim that sometimes this word designates Ahasuerus, and other times God. The Hebrew word for "king" is in fact also one of the names of God, and we find it on several occasions in Esther's responses (5:4,8; 7:3). Might she not then be talking about God?

Following this suggestion, we can make a layered reading of Esther's responses. On one level we discover an apparently submissive wife who is even friendly toward Haman. Although she defers her request, it is not a matter of her shying away. She simply imposes a momentary pause, a kind of void, which serves as a destabilizing time, as chapter 6 shows. But the delicacy and finesse with which she twice puts off explaining herself to the next day, allow the two men to comply with her will without losing face. Even more, Haman thinks he has become one of the queen's favorites.

On a second level there opens up for us the hidden face of Esther, a completely different woman who knows that, in order to save the Jews from extermination, she has to work in harmony with God. So she is anxious to put both banquets into God's hands.

Ahasuerus and Haman are invited not only to come to a banquet with the queen but to appear before her God as well. For Esther's response (5:8) can be read thus: "If I have won the king's (= God's) favor, and if it pleases the king (= God) to grant my petition and fulfill my request, let the king (= Ahasuerus) and Haman come tomorrow to the banquet that I will prepare for them, and then I will do as the king has said." Ahasuerus will have his answer and the will of God will be respected.

The next day when the king and his chief minister come to sit down at the banquet, Esther's fast is over, and Ahasuerus asks a third time what his wife's request is. As she had promised, she answers: "If I have won your favor, O king (= God), and if it pleases the king (= Ahasuerus), let my life be given me—that is my petition—and the lives of my people—that is my request" (7:3).

TACT AND REALISM

Esther knew that her response would shock her husband. It is a startling revelation to learn that the woman with whom he had shared his life for more than nine years is a Jew, a woman belonging to a people he had condemned to extermination. So she asks that she not be put to death and only after that for the salvation of her people. She shows great tact in acting this way, for she knows his love for her. Has he not just promised her anything up to half of his kingdom? By arousing the king's interest in her own life first, she thinks she has more chances of obtaining the safety of her people afterward. And then she describes Haman's action as a misdeed that undermines the king as well (7:4). For it had been prophesied that the Jews would be reduced to slavery, but never does Torah predict their complete extermination. If that happened, the king would have to expect a terrible punishment.

Banquets of supplication, banquets of the revelation of a hidden God: these are the kinds of banquets to which Esther has invited Ahasuerus and Haman.

Jewish interpretation makes us more attentive to the form that Esther uses in her invitation: "let the king and Haman come today" (5:4). The first letters of these words in Hebrew form the name of God, YHWH, which gives a very special connotation to Esther's banquets. It is not just a matter of meals with friends but of encounters where God is invited to take a place in the march of history. Two kings, two powers face to face! It can be said in this case that the earthly king is only a puppet in the heavenly king's hand.

The usual commentaries often speak of Esther's behavior as trickery. I see instead a very feminine way of dealing with the patriarchal system. Esther moves forward step by step. She creates encounters and dialogues with her banquets; she forges links. She acts taking account of the different psychologies of Ahasuerus and of Haman. Her tactics take into consideration her husband's jealousy and vanity as well as Haman's pride, arrogance, and especially his racist hatred. Esther is not a cunning woman in the pejorative sense of the word. She is a perspicacious realist whose wisdom is marked by patience, delicacy, and determination all at the same time.

WHEN HISTORY REVERSES ITSELF

The seventh and last banquet that the book of Esther has us attend is the one that the exiled Jews organize in order to celebrate their deliverance and thank God for having altered the course of events (9:17). This banquet, according to Mordecai's wish, is to be observed every year by days of general rejoicing (9:22, 27). This is the feast of Purim.

However, we often say that Purim leaves us with a bitter taste. Considering the final banquet, it is impossible not to experience divided feelings. So much violence, so many innocents killed because they belong to the other side. Certainly, Jewish exegesis clarifies, the reprisals against the inhabitants of Susa are not undertaken blindly. The Jews take care to discern who are really their enemies, those who by showing their hatred openly declare themselves anti-Semites, of the spiritual family of Amalek. On the other hand those who hate them with only an inner hatred, certainly terrible but not going so far as to commit murderous acts, these are only humiliated and not massacred like the others.

In addition we notice that the permission given to the Jews to defend their life by arms is duly announced to them by royal edict, as well as to the men in charge of the hundred twenty-seven provinces, and that it is limited in time besides: "a single day." It also included the detail not to help oneself to spoils (8:9–13), a provision that distances it from the preceding decree, inspired by Haman, which had been vague and secret likely in order to engender fear, and which allowed the appropriation of all the Jews' goods (3:12–13).

We have an unsettled feeling after reading the story of Esther. Even considering some right of self-defense on the part of the Jews of Susa, the use of physical force here seems more like a failure in human relations. Besides, evil is not neutralized. It is only that the people in whom evil appears to dwell die violent deaths.

For my part I do not find a satisfying explanation for the violence of the book of Esther. This is just as well, for one cannot turn violence into a theory and give lessons on it. Nevertheless, we cannot put aside a subject of such topicality under the pretext that it disturbs us. But since I do not feel I have the right to say a word because it would be the word of an outsider, I cede my place to the Jewish witness par excellence, Elie Wiesel, whose reflections on war and violence can, I hope, help readers in their personal reflections.

WAR IS NEVER WHOLESOME

In a chapter of his book *Paroles d'étranger* Wiesel writes:

> When men make war, God is their first victim. This is why the prophets are always inveighing against the king's policy of war; they cannot make their counsels of prudence, patience, moderation, pacifism, and faith in God strong enough. War is never a blessing for Israel. The Bible does set out the warrior exploits of Saul, David, Samson, Judas Maccabeus, and Bar Kokhba. The texts recount these exploits proudly, but they are never given as examples.
>
> The Talmud is never ashamed of reproaching David for certain battles it judges not absolutely necessary. Of the eighteen wars David engaged in, only thirteen were for Israel's good. The others he engaged in for his own glory. . . Our war generals are rarely saints. The two terms placed alongside each other reveal the blasphemy. . . Killing, even if it is for a superior cause, diminishes man. . . In the eyes of Jewish tradition, war is never salutary.[1]

Compared with these words, the end of the book of Esther seems to stand as a contradiction. And it is apparently not alone in countering Wiesel's thesis. He writes that there is also the Warsaw ghetto revolt.

> On the evening of April 19, 1943, the uprising only just begun, the Jewish combatants are congratulating each

1. Wiesel, *Paroles d'étranger*, 114.

other, embracing each other, laughing and weeping for joy. The sight of the German corpses fills them with pride and happiness. Well, do not judge them too quickly. We cannot judge victims or heroes from a distance. These young men and women who wore their Jewish destiny on their shoulders in those days have not denied their tradition. Do not see in their behavior a thirst for vengeance or the satisfaction of base instincts. Their momentary ecstasy had nothing to do with the men lying in their own blood; their motives were different. For months and years, the Germans strutted about the alleys of the ghetto like invincible and immortal gods; this was the impression that consciously and deliberately they wanted to produce, and due to undergoing fear, hunger, due to being drowned in death, the Jews had sometimes come to believe it. Oh yes, in the kingdom of the Night it was easy to conclude that God was the enemy. Or worse yet, that the enemy was God.

And now, April 19, 1943, the killer is wounded, howling with grief, in the throes of death, as vulnerable and as mortal as his victims. That evening after the first engagement the Jews realized that the killer was not God, that he was human, mortal. That is why they gave free rein to their enthusiasm. They were happy, not only for having killed the enemy but also for having unmasked and demythologized him.[2]

Between the 13 and 14 of Adar, the Jews of Susa slaughtered many anti-Semites. Did they thereby discover, as later many of their brothers and sisters at Warsaw would discover, that it was not God who desired their death, but a human being, Haman, and that he, like them was mortal? Who could doubt that?

If we can put forward this way of understanding the joyous final banquet, then Esther and Mordecai, the symbolic authors of the Megillah, would be the ancestors of the chroniclers and historians, of all the Wiesels of every age who, in order to "prevent the enemy from writing the history of his victim, are anxious to

2. Wiesel, *Paroles d'étranger*, 128–29.

recount their experience so that it might serve as a warning. They valued not so much living, as continuing to live."[3]

The unsettled feeling we have after reading the story of Esther is probably not surprising when we remember that *Purim* derives from *Kippurim*, the Day of Atonement. This keeps us attentive to the ascendancy of Yom Kippur over Purim. Yom Kippur is the solemn day annually set aside "to cleanse [the people] from all [their] sins" (Lev 16:30) and, as Jewish tradition has it, all creation once again returns to its primeval order.

3. Wiesel, *Paroles d'étranger*, 129.

3

Two Women—Agents of Change

IN THE FEASTS WHICH serve as a framework for the book of Esther, two women play a central role, Vashti the rebel and Esther the exile. We have already noted how different their ways of acting and their strategies were. It remains now to bring out some elements that will let us better understand the originality and impact of their lives.

VASHTI THE REBEL

Although without a large presence in the narrative, Vashti neverthe-less plays a decisive role. In fact without her, without her rebellion, there would not have been a Queen Esther, there would not have been a story, and by that token there would not be a feast of Purim.

Vashti is active only in the first chapter of the book, in the two banquets offered to the people of Susa. According to Lucie Bolens, at issue here is "the presentation of a royal couple, divin-ized in the manner of Egyptian royal couples, probably in a ritual that speaks of a cosmic seclusion of six months connected to the ancient appearance of the couple as guarantors in the heavens of cosmic equilibrium. Each of their faces, both the king's and the queen's, is spoken of in the plural, rather like the double face of Janus of old, and like the stars with rays moving according to the time of year or month."[1]

During these memorable banquets, Vashti is invited to show her beauty, and we have seen that her categorical refusal provokes a shaking of the foundations, a shaking of the patriarchal system itself. Still according to Lucie Bolens, Vashti's "no" involves "a movement of deep emotion among the guardians of the official cosmology, the sages 'who were versed in law and custom' (Esth 1:13–15). The astrologers in fact have responsibility for the world, and lack of respect for the cosmic order has its effects on society, as the text says (Esth 1:16)."[2]

A VERITABLE REVOLUTION

Vashti's rebellion disturbs both the religious order and the social order. We meet such rituals elsewhere. The exhibition of beauty and female nudity appear in the medieval ritual of the Lay of Graelent. On Pentecost every year the king calls his barons together. After the banquet, they would have the queen placed on an elevated couch and then order her to undress. Upon her complying, he would say to the assembly, "My lord barons, what does it seem to you? Is there under heaven a queen, a woman, lady or girl, more beautiful than she?"

This is the ritual in which Vashti refused to participate. It causes her only repugnance, and she is fearless of the consequences. Her dignity as a woman counts more for her than the established order. She is a rebel!

The Hebrew text, which calls her sometimes Vashti the queen and sometimes Queen Vashti, allows us to examine one aspect of the patriarchal strategy. The two ways of expressing her identity reflect perfectly the mentality of the court at Susa regarding women.

---

1. Bolens, *La Bible et l'histoire au féminin*, 83.
2. Bolens, *La Bible et l'histoire*, 84.

When Ahasuerus has her brought in so that she may undress before the noble assemblage, she is called Vashti the queen. We can see a certain contempt here (1:9, 11, 16, 17b). It implies that her title is of secondary importance; she is a Vashti, a woman raised to royalty by the good pleasure of the king. She sees herself treated not as a woman, but as a beautiful object that can be admired at leisure, as long as the admirers do not forget to envy the owner of that beautiful object!

Presumably the king did not expect that his wife would refuse to "moon" his guests just to choose simply to be a woman. The text says, "Queen Vashti refused" (1:12), thus underlining the fact that she does not permit anyone to play with her dignity or her identity. The granddaughter of Nebuchadnezzar is not just anybody!

So when Ahasuerus speaks of her as Queen Vashti (vv. 12, 15, 17a), he is announcing her place in the cosmic order, her role as divinized queen, and highlighting her culpability in questioning the role which had devolved upon her. She commits an unpardonable offense which reduces her to being no more than Vashti, an object—a woman whom one does not hesitate to banish in order to replace her with a woman of greater worth (1:19). This will be the role of Esther who, and notice this well, succeeds Vashti under a similar lunar identity since, according to Rashi, her name Ishtar means "as beautiful as the moon."

Vashti's rebellion is fundamental insofar as it provokes a wholesale revolution. Her successor will no longer incarnate simply lunar beauty, but the feminine form of the divine as well. Esther is not necessarily worth more than Vashti; she will not necessarily be a better wife for the king (cf. 1:19). She will be radically different. Certainly she is also a radiant beauty, but hers is a beauty that expresses itself in gratuitous love and in the strength of her goodness. Vashti's insubordination allows Esther to raise her beauty into the ranks of ethics, of the good.

THE HIDDEN ESTHER

Esther had a splendid body and a handsome face; she was "fair and beautiful," as we are told (2:7). While her physical person raises no question in particular, her twofold name, Ishtar in Babylonian, Hadassah in Hebrew, poses numerous questions indeed. The sages never could come to agreement on which was her true and original name.

If the explanations are many, they can complement each other rather than be exclusive. Ishtar could be the Babylonian name which was given her when she became empress of Persia. As we just saw, this name according to Rashi means "as beautiful as the moon," a meaning with obvious lunar connotation. Also the name Esther/Ishtar can come from the Hebrew root "str" which means to hide, to secrete away. And the name Hadassah means myrtle in Hebrew.

Two names, two facets of one personality—about one a midrash suggests: "Just as myrtle has a good smell and a bitter taste, so Esther was good for Mordecai but bitter for Haman." About the other, her life itself unravels like a game of hide and seek between her being shut up in the harem and her outings for official celebrations. Yes, Esther lives her name well as she manages to hide her identity as a Jewish woman from her husband and the whole court for five years (1:10, 16, 20; 3:17).

A text from the Zohar, the principal work of Jewish mysticism, helps us better understand the complexity of the role Esther played. It recounts how as God "verged on creating the world, all the letters presented themselves" and offered themselves as the vehicles of creation. The letter *tav*, the last letter of the alphabet, presented herself first. For reasons best known to the divine mind, God rejects all the letters, except the first two, *aleph* and *beth*. To *beth* "the Holy One replied, 'Indeed, by you I will create the world. You will be the beginning of Creation.'" Addressing *aleph*, which had begun modestly in the last row of the candidates, God said, "'Although I will create the world with the letter *beth*, you will be the first of all the letters. Only through you do I become one. With you all counting begins and every deed in the world. No union is actualized except by *aleph*."[3]

In Hebrew the first letter of the name Esther is an *aleph*. In Jewish tradition we know that one's name represents not only the person's identity but also the life program to which that person will be dedicated. We can therefore deduce that Mordecai chose Esther as wife, spouse, house, but especially as his partner in the arduous task while in exile of putting God's projects into effect. And God in turn chose her to make her his instrument in putting things in order and holding Haman's diabolical plan in check.

FREE TO BE HERSELF

While this woman's beauty certainly fascinated Ahasuerus, who made her a great empress, we women are more fascinated by the complexity of her personality and by her inner beauty.

In fact it is remarkable to see how she knew, insofar as she was a woman, how to maintain her female differentness. Throughout her story we see her as difference personified. She is a female counterpart both for and against her male opposite number, whether Ahasuerus or Mordecai. She behaves as an autonomous woman at the heart of patriarchal structures, and she manages to make free choices in spite of her status as an exile, a captive. She remains deeply Jewish in the inspiration of her actions and united with her people, while assuming her role as empress at the head of a foreign kingdom.

Esther knows how to place and maintain herself interiorly and within her identity as a woman, a Jewish woman. At the same time she adapts to the events of history without ever denying one or the other facet of her identity, allowing her to develop a strategy of freedom. Therefore she is not only a model for women but also a figure of modernity, a source of inspiration combining intelligence, intuition, and firmness in a new harmony. Esther lives and loves with all her heart, with all her being, with all her strength.

3. *The Zohar*, 11–16.

4

The Dynamic of Disobedience

As THE STORY OF Esther develops, disobedience appears to be one of the principal driving forces. We have already seen that Vashti's rebellion sets the whole adventure in motion. She is not however the only one to use her freedom in that way. In order to remain faithful to their roots and faith, Esther and Mordecai will also choose the way of disobedience.

FORCED TO BE A WIFE

In the Greek version of the book we read that the royal role is more of a burden than a privilege for Esther. She does not hesitate to compare the royal crown, the symbol of her elevation to this high rank, to a sanitary napkin. This "sign of [her] proud position" disgusts her so much that she wears it only on days when functions absolutely demand it (Gk Esth C.14:16). Her position at the head of the kingdom has not made her lose her sense of reality, but she does not know how fragile she remains. Is she forgetting Vashti's fate?

Forced to become Ahasuerus's wife, she is very much still, as she herself emphasizes, the daughter of Abihail (Esth 2:15). She belongs to a family, to a history that links her forever to a peculiar people, the Jewish people. Queen of Persia, she keeps her roots and identity deeply anchored within herself. She even makes them a secret that she refuses to divulge. Acting in this way, she is choosing a dangerous role. She is disobeying the king. And Mordecai makes the same choice with respect to Haman. With all the risks it entails, Esther will force herself to reconcile the irreconcilables— she will remain faithful to Mordecai and her people and rule at Ahasuerus's side at the same time.

At this time in the region of Susa, the Jews were admittedly not suffering excessively. Several of them had even risen to important political and economic positions. Mordecai himself certainly belongs among these privileged ones who, like Joseph in the court of Pharaoh, participate in the life of the nation where history has placed them. The story of Esther teaches us that this kind of adaptation to surrounding society has its limits though, and Mordecai is a good example of this.

MORDECAI'S REFUSAL

The royal decree demanding that all subjects bow down to and worship the chief royal official was unacceptable to Mordecai. He becomes disobedient in turn and refuses categorically to do it (3:1–2). This open form of revolt against the established order does not go unnoticed by the courtiers who ask him what impels him to behave this way. He responds simply by telling them he is a Jew (3:4), that as a Jew he is bound to reserve such acts for God alone. This refusal throws Haman's power into question. It is a religious decision of course, but its political meaning is no less evident. After Vashti, it appears to be Mordecai's turn to contest this cult of personality.

Haman understands perfectly. His reaction to this personal insult, of which he feels the victim, is characteristic of despots, as well as characteristic of the most ardent anti-Semites through the ages. Instead of targeting only the individual concerned, Mordecai, Haman decides to annihilate not just the Jews of the Persian

Empire, but the entire Jewish nation. His conduct prefigures what from the era of World War II has been called "the final solution."

We saw it in the case of Vashti—when disobedience touches the foundations of the patriarchy, that is, of arbitrary power, the reaction is always on the order of violent extermination. Difference cannot be tolerated; it must be destroyed at all costs. Vashti was summarily divorced. Some Jewish commentators even say she was executed. Mordecai, and his people with him, must take their turn and be exterminated by Haman's murderous response.

In its way the book of Esther furnishes the answer to the question of how to behave in the face of totalitarian power. Without ambiguity Mordecai chooses to obey Torah rather than a decree that obliges him to deny what, for him, is an essential aspect of his faith.

Vashti, a woman, unmasks the strength of patriarchy vs. the fragility of women. Mordecai, a Jew, denounces royal power in the name of what, for him, is a higher power, the power of God. Thus disobedience becomes a confrontation of two powers, of two completely incompatible outlooks on life. On the one hand, there are Ahasuerus and Haman who want to bring all women and Jews to their knees, and on the other Vashti and Mordecai, representing the humiliated, those who dare to say no and insist on their right to be free to be themselves.

At first sight Haman seems to be the victor since the king assents to abandoning the Jews to his pleasure and even refuses the bribe of ten thousand pieces of silver that Haman offers as compensation for the loss of tax revenue that the execution of the Jews would cause (3:9–11). At this point in the story the rhythm accelerates briskly. Couriers are sent at high speed to the four corners of the kingdom to order the massacre of the Jews (3:15). Ahasuerus must not be allowed to change his mind. Therefore, once the edict was published, the king and his minister can celebrate quietly and toast the projected elimination of the Jews. But while the court is in a gay mood, the city of Susa, and especially its Jewish residents, are in consternation.

During these events in which her people's fate is in play, Esther, shut up inside the palace, is in total ignorance of what is happening outside. How well she bears the name of "the hidden Esther," she from whom the publication of the royal decree and the desolating sadness of the Jews are hidden!

In the midst of the turmoil Mordecai resorted to the traditional ways of showing his sorrow: sackcloth and ashes and wailing (4:1). When Esther is at last informed, she is deeply bewildered. She sends clothing to Mordecai so that he can take off his sackcloth, but he refuses. That is when through the mediation of a eunuch she learns that Mordecai's disobedience has provoked a catastrophe for her people. She obtains a copy of the decree, and when she does, Mordecai appeals to her to move the king to have mercy on their people (4:4–9).

COMPLYING WITH THE RULES

Mordecai's request plunges Esther into great perplexity, for what is wanted from her now would force her to transgress the rule that forbids anyone, even the queen, to approach the king unless he calls for them. It is possible that at this moment she is thinking about what happened to Vashti. She does not want to risk her life without hedging her bets.

When she sends Mordecai her decision, her refusal to accede to his request, Esther takes the opportunity to explain to him the situation that prevails inside the palace, what in fact a woman's life is like in a patriarchal structure (4:10–16). She has not been called into the king's presence for a month. However, she does not think that this silence is synonymous with being cast aside. There is no indication that she will not be invited soon; then she will more easily be able to take the opportunity to intercede in behalf of her people. Besides, she has to keep in mind the shock Ahasuerus will undergo when he learns that his wife is a Jew. Would Mordecai have forgotten his recommendation at the time of her marriage that she keep her identity as a Jew quiet? It is not truly possible for Esther, in these circumstances, to defy the law. Such a provocation would probably entail her death without at all guaranteeing the welfare of her people.

Esther's response perfectly underscores the absurdity of the situation that holds her prisoner. Although the wife of the king, she is not free to approach him when she wants. She depends for everything on his goodwill and knows she is constrained to comply with the rules of the harem. This is not self-regard, but realism. She cherishes no illusions. She does not even imagine that as queen she might escape the condemnation that threatens her people. As a woman she also knows from the inside the rules that govern the female condition. She has been accustomed to playing by them for a long time. She knows what has to be done better than Mordecai does.

ESTHER'S "THIRD DAY"

So Esther chooses the tactic of temporizing. Before engaging negotiators and risking her life, she wants to hedge her bets carefully. Sensing the need to know how she stands in all this with herself, with her God, and with her people, she gives herself a time for reflection. She decides on three days and three nights of fasting, first for herself, but also for her servants and for the whole Jewish people. In disobeying Mordecai and proclaiming a fast, she writes herself into the lineage of the prophets. With this three days of testing, she takes on the biblical requirement for any hope for deliverance, any hope for a return to life.

In Jewish exegesis the expression "the third day" is used in a particular sense. It is the day that marks the end of a time of testing, as we read in the book of the prophet Hosea: "After two days he will revive us; on the third day he will raise us up, that we may live before him" (Hos 6:2). In the same sense midrashic tradition evokes the "third day" of Abraham (Gen 22:4), the "third day" of the children of Jacob (Gen 34:25–31), the "third day" of the revelation on Mount Sinai (Exod 19:16), the "third day" of the spies (Josh 2:16), the "third day" of Jonah (Jon 2:1), the "third day" of the return from exile (Ez 8:32), and finally the "third day" of Esther (Esth 5:1).

This expression turns up again in the Second Testament applied most often to the third day of Jesus, the day of his resurrection (Matt 16:21; 17:23; 20:19; 27:64; Luke 24:7, 46; Ac 10:40; 1 Cor 15:4; cf. also Matt 12:39–40). Three texts are exceptions. At issue in the first is the finding of the boy Jesus in the temple after three days (Luke 2:46). "After three days they found him in the temple, sitting among the teachers, listening to them and asking them questions."

The second is the third day of the disciples of Emmaus (Luke 24:21). Astonished, they point out the fact that "it is now the third day since these things took place," and nothing more decisive had happened to put an end to their ordeal, their sadness. It is only toward the end of this "third day," and by Jesus' gesture of breaking of bread, that they are "raised up" and that they can "live before him," in the words of Hosea cited above.

The third exception concerns the "third day" of Mary: "On the third day there was a wedding in Cana of Galilee, and the mother of Jesus was there" (John 2:1). These words are often interpreted, because they appear unexpectedly, as having to do with the custom of marrying on the third day of the week. But it can bear another interpretation as well, one that does not exclude the other—at Cana Jesus, at the instigation of his mother, performs his first sign, thus ending what must have been for Mary a long period of inner questioning about her son. The public sign at Cana marks a turning point in her life. The ordeal of doubt is over.

STANDING, IN SPITE OF EVERYTHING

But we return to Esther. For her the "third day" is the one on which she arrays herself in her royal vesture (5:1). Mordecai has scrupulously performed what she directed him to do. The fast is not completely over, yet the moment has come for her to go to the king. The woman who is daring enough to take the initiative of such a dangerous step has just spent two days and a half in the presence of God, clothed in "garments of distress and mourning . . . her head [covered] with ashes and dung" (Add Esth C:14:2.)

37

Esther's long prayer, reported in the Greek text, shows the different aspects of exile that she endures. Far from her family, in this foreign palace, she must live according to strange customs without however participating wholly in them. In her solitude she forces herself to safeguard her difference, to maintain a space of freedom in her daily life. However small that space might be, it allows her to return continually to the truth of her being and to the hidden presence of her God.

Clothed with all the exterior signs of royalty, Esther pursues her path on the way of disobedience. This third day in fact, according to Rashi, falls on the first day of the feast of Passover. In spite of this feast, or rather because of the hope of liberation which it expresses, Esther finds the strength, on so solemn a day, to wear her royal garments that inspire such disgust in her.

How do we understand such behavior? Once again, the midrash furnishes an answer for us. We have just seen that the "third day" is a day unlike all others. It is the day on which to get back on one's feet in order to live in the presence of God (Hos 6:2). Therefore, the sumptuous vesture with which Esther is clothed symbolizes this change. Clothed with the Holy Spirit, taking part in a royalty of an entirely other order, she will defy the king's injunction.

The king saw Esther, supported by God himself and "standing in the court," as the text makes clear (Esth 5:2). Standing is however not the usual position for a person requesting a favor! But in the Bible standing is the posture of prayer, which from Esther does not surprise us. Is she not clothed with the Holy Spirit as the midrash says? Has she not acquired the conviction that God alone can save her, just as that God alone can save her people? Facing the king, she remains standing, that is, she stops to pray.

The course of history then reverses itself. Ahasuerus holds out his golden scepter to her. Esther may approach and touch it. Not only did the king not become angry, but he is even worried about his wife's health and asks her what is wrong (5:3). Perhaps her fast has made her pale.

A DESTABILIZING MOMENT

After the tension and fear that Esther has just lived through, we expect that she will explain without delay the motive of her bold disobedience. She does nothing however. She leaves the question unanswered and invites the king and his minister Haman to the banquet that she has had prepared for them. In this way she submits to the customs of the country and places their meeting within the character of conviviality (5:4).

In the course of the meal Ahasuerus realizes that his wife has not risked her life for the simple pleasure of eating with him and his chief official. Therefore he asks her a second time what she wants from him. And for the second time Esther ignores the question and repeats her invitation to share another meal with her the next day (5:6–8).

So before answering, Esther leaves herself room for freedom and puts forth her conditions. By inviting Haman, she stops him from plotting. By postponing her response to the king, she opens up a space of time that is both destabilizing and revealing. By temporizing, she makes herself mistress of the situation. Not only does she not conform to Mordecai's orders and suggestions, she even makes her royal and bad-tempered husband wait. When we think of the speed with which Vashti met her disgrace, this astonishing sequence of events emphasizes the strength and authority of Esther's personality. Her will is understood and accepted by the king and his entourage.

In the meantime they each get ready, in their own way, for the next banquet. Haman, who believes he has arrived at the pinnacle of his glory and who tells everywhere that he is the only one to be invited with the king to the queen's banquet, decides to be done once and for all with Mordecai. The liberty this Jew takes in disobeying him has become intolerable for his proud nature. He can no longer stand to see him seated in the king's gate taunting his authority. So he spends the night erecting a gallows because his wife Zeresh pointed out that not a single Jew was ever known to have been saved from hanging. This is at least the explanation that a midrash gives for his choice of instrument of revenge (see Esth 5:9–14).

Esther in Exile

While Haman plays at being a carpenter, the king vainly tries to sleep (61). This night is a night unlike other nights. In our story this night symbolizes the struggle against the powers of death, the struggle between Mordecai and Haman, between light and dark. It is reminiscent of another night, the night in the course of which God traversed the country of Egypt and personally effected the salvation of the Hebrews (Exod 12:12).

THE KING'S INSOMNIA

Ahasuerus suffers from insomnia. This remark can be read in another way. The king is literally subject to sleeping troubles. But we have already noted that the name of God, absent from the book of Esther, can be replaced with the word "king." There is nothing stopping us then from reading this to mean that it is God, not Ahasuerus, who suffers from insomnia.

Various passages in the midrash adopt this meaning. Here is one: After having completed the construction of the gallows, Haman goes to Mordecai. He finds him in the house of studies with his pupils. They were dressed in sackcloth and studying Torah and were weeping and wailing. Haman counted twenty-two thousand and put them in chains. He set a guard and announced that on the next day he would kill the young men first, then Mordecai. The mothers who brought bread and water say: "Children, eat and drink, for tomorrow you will die. Stop your fast." At these words the young men put their hands on their books and swore on their master Mordecai's life that they would neither eat nor drink and would die fasting. Their lamentations were such that they reached to heaven, and the Holy One, blessed be he, heard the noise. It was the second hour of the night. At the same time his compassion was awakened, and he left the throne of justice and sat on the throne of mercy and said: "What is this great noise like the bleating of young lambs?" Our master Moses stood before the Holy One, blessed be he, and said: "Master of the universe, it is not the bleating of young lambs you hear, but the children of your people who have been fasting three days and three nights, for tomorrow their throats will be cut like young lambs." Hearing this, the Holy One, blessed be he, took the death decrees, broke the seals, and after tearing them up, he let the pieces fall on Ahasuerus in the middle of the night, as it is written: "this same night . . ."

Interpreted this way, the insomnia of the "king" concerns God personally. He is moved and troubled. The fast, accompanied by lamentation and repentance, shakes him to the point of making him change thrones, and his trouble is so great that he communicates it to Ahasuerus himself.

In the book of Esther God is hidden, but not deaf. As it is written: "God heard their groaning, and God remembered his covenant with Abraham, Isaac, and Jacob. God looked upon the Israelites, and God took notice of them" (Exod 2:24–25). Truly this night is not like any other night. It resembles strangely the night preceding the departure from Egypt.

When God's problem is communicated to Ahasuerus, it is however another command. Like every authoritarian monarch Ahasuerus is assailed with the fear of plots. Has not someone already tried to assassinate him (Esth 2:22–23)? That escape was due to Mordecai's vigilance. On the other hand he is preoccupied with Esther's behavior. Why has she twice deferred an answer to his question? And why does she invite Haman to each banquet. Was there some sort of liaison between them of which he was unaware?

In order to calm his fears, Ahasuerus asks to be read to from the book of the annals, a way of recalling the events of preceding years. That is when he discovers Mordecai had never been compensated for saving his life (6:1–3).

CAUGHT IN HIS OWN TRAP

The rest of the story can be considered as a parable. Without apparent reason the king asks who is in the courtyard (6:4). This is one of those literary "empty spaces," and we have seen how the midrash interprets them. Ahasuarus's sudden question shows what is troubling him. Therefore, when he finds out that his first minister is in the courtyard, he has him sent for immediately. And we find ourselves in attendance upon a quid pro quo that reverses roles and turns worlds upside down.

Haman who comes asking the king for Mordecai's death, while planning to rid the empire of all these troublesome Jews, has no doubt that the person the king wishes to honor is himself. So he does not hesitate to propose the highest distinctions (6:6–9). Then of course he is dumbfounded to hear Mordecai's name pronounced, that Jew who defies him day after day by refusing to bow down to him. However, he cannot reverse events, and we find ourselves present at the start of his fall, forced to accompany his worst enemy wearing the royal collar through the streets of Susa.

This reversal reminds us of another quid pro quo, that encounter of David with Nathan (2 Sam 12:1–14). Whereas David has sense enough to understand the prophet's lesson and repent, Haman remains deaf to the warning. He perseveres in his plan for revenge, and the hate that blinds him precipitates his ruin. His wife is more perceptive and understands the situation right away. She has no hesitation in telling him: "If Mordecai, before whom your downfall has begun, is of the Jewish people, you will not prevail against him, but will surely fall before him" (6:13). This is an argument tailor made for the anti-Semites—"If Mordecai . . . is of the Jewish people . . ." But from Zeresh's mouth the remark is at the very least ambiguous. On the one hand she seems to be announcing her husband's downfall, but on the other hand she might be encouraging him to persist to the end with his plan of extermination.

As for Mordecai, after having received the king's honors, he returned to his seat at the royal gate and continued his fast of protest. It seems he is disappointed, for he certainly would have preferred the annulment of the death decree as compensation for his services (6:12).

5

Collaborating with God

As we can note in the overall trajectory of the First Testament, the expectation of a liberator developed over time in Judaism. The concept of a messiah takes shape little by little and assumes the characteristics of prophet and priest and king.

A FEMALE MESSIAH

But can the unusual idea of a female messiah be applied to Esther? As we know, she had two names. Hadassah, her Hebrew name, means myrtle, a plant used in Jewish betrothal rituals. Its leaves are also used in the construction of the booths for Succoth (Neh 8:15). In addition, its therapeutic powers make it useful in the preparation of medicines. So it is both a symbol of love and a symbol of health. Esther, her other name, begins with the letter *aleph*, with widely known mystical meanings in Jewish tradition all the way from the oneness of God to human qualities of goodness and tenderness rolled into one. Hadassah, Esther, two names, two life plans, which make our heroine a collaborator of God, chosen as a foundation stone for the healing and liberation of her people.

Through her three days of testing, Esther fully assumes her responsibility as a human being. Chosen for a specific task, she in turn chooses God as the only one who can allow her to bring her mission to a successful conclusion: to save her people from death. This is how she brings the dimension of healing into the very heart of exile in her attempt to transform the ordeal of exile into a time of redemption. A traditional teaching suggests that the difference between the Hebrew words for exile and redemption is the presence of the *aleph*. If an *aleph* is inserted into (the word for) exile, exile received power to be transformed into (the word for) redemption. Tradition therefore regards *aleph* as a great gift of God.

One of Esther's great merits is her tireless search for the face of this hidden God. She examines events in an almost defiant fashion in order to discover their hidden meaning. Exile becomes for her an immense challenge within which she finds a new way of being Jewish, of making visible the two vocations inscribed in her two names.

Perhaps this explains why she turns to disobedience and revolt. But she does so in a way that reflects her inmost being. Her revolt is not violent. It is the exact opposite, and she is all about grace and subtlety and patience and tenderness. She gives prayer, fasting, and conversation first place. She does not place her trust in her high position as queen but to it prefers submission to God, even if God remains silent.

The difficult apprenticeship of exile thus permits her to discover that she is not like others, but for others. Her disobedience is transformed into fundamental obedience to Torah so that then God can act through her. She will save her people because she has been bold enough to stake everything on the presence of this hidden God.

BENEATH THE COALS, A SPARK OF LIFE

The book of Esther teaches us that God is revealed fully only in close collaboration with a human being. God's engagement with history requires our engagement with history as well. What an inexhaustible mystery this divine decision is! God needs us after all. Esther understood this fundamental aspect of the human vocation. She consented to enter into this demanding partnership, which she actually found exhilarating. Liberty and constraint, hope and anguish are the framework of her life as an exile, and her people's situation demands a sacrifice from her, perhaps the sacrifice of her life. But she is not unaware that the only possible hope of salvation is fitted into this sacrifice, like a diamond into its mounting.

Plunged into the darkness of exile, into the night of an anti-Semitic world, she rediscovers the Jewish vocation, the founding experience of the Passover. In her way, in her way as a woman, she clears a pathway that leads to the other side. Her disobedience is etched into the great tradition of Abraham and Sarah and the prophets—protesting and breaking with all the towers of Babel. There were many gods at Susa, many material, cultural, and religious riches, but Esther has chosen the better part, that of a hidden God who lets himself be found.

Esther's wager on life makes her a modern messianic figure. She inaugurates a female project of hope, a project that is always called for when faced with the Amaleks of history. By creating a paschal pathway for the exiles of Babylon, she shows that exile is not a dead-end street or a fate worse than death, but that at the very heart of the darkest events there hides, like the fire in the embers, a spark of life powerful enough to set a whole people on their feet.

Esther has searched for this spark at the most elemental level, in her day-to-day life. And in the end she found it in faithfulness to herself and to God, in an interdependence that is both horizontal and vertical. She knew how to be a woman with Ahasuerus, with Mordecai, and with her people, without ever ceasing to be true to herself.

In a particular time, but one that strangely resembles our own and when God seems astonishingly absent, Esther had the experience that God is all in all, and that all is in God as well. It is not an unusual experience after all, for do we not have similar experiences in our own struggles and questionings?

THE COURAGE TO CONFRONT

Is it really possible to remain beings of flesh and blood, passion and compassion in the struggle for life and survival? Like "a roaring lion," a life-threatening force "prowls around, looking for someone to devour" (1 Pet 5:8). War, violence, racism, sexism, marginalization, oppression, deportation are daily realities for many today. But these expanding forces of death are found not only around us, but within us as well. We meet them both in our personal life and in the life of society. The challenge is how to preserve a heart of flesh, how to remain open and vulnerable and not cede to the temptation of indifference or insensitivity that would turn our hearts to stone.

If in the face of absolute, totalitarian evil, Esther and Mordecai resorted to disobedience and violence, in their personal life they preferred to confront events with their hearts in order to try to learn from them and not destroy each other. To arrive at that point, they employ the technique of dialogue. In different forms this dialogue, like Jacob's ladder, will allow them to keep in touch with heaven and with earth and with each other as well. This continuous coming and going between the here and now and the then and there, between the outer and the inner, this is the dialogical path which Esther and Mordecai chose in order to sanctify life.

DIALOGUE BETWEEN THE INNER
AND THE OUTER

Inside the harem Esther's life is that of a recluse. All communication with the outer world is cut off. Mordecai is not resigned to dealing with that circumstance. Every day he walks up and down the approaches to the harem in order to catch some news of the prisoner. In the form of a nonverbal dialogue he maintains relations with the exterior and interior of the palace (2:11).

Mordecai is certainly solicitous of the wellbeing of his wife, but he is equally strongly preoccupied by the thought he had had a year earlier but had kept secret. It had been revealed to him that when his people would be on the verge of annihilation, a cry would mount to heaven. Bursting out of a tiny spring, this cry would be transformed into a broad river, into flowing water. Another light would rise in addition to the sun, and the humble and meek would be exalted while the nobles of the land would disappear (Add Esth A 11:10–12).

This dream had never left him, and at the time of Esther's sequestration it took on a particular resonance. By reflecting on it and comparing it with the reality of their situation, Mordecai arrived at the conclusion that if ever Esther was chosen as queen, as paradoxical as it was sad, the dream would become reality. Would Esther be this light alongside the sun that will save the exiles?

So it is of first importance that Mordecai maintain communication with the inside of the palace in order to assess the worth of his intuition. This is why, as discreetly as possible, he searches for news each day. Simply to survive in exile, it does not do to be too much noticed, and it is better to keep certain things secret. They are carried within, measured against daily realities, their meaning carefully discerned. One keeps them as part of an inner dialogue capable at any time of fueling a growing sense of hope.

It is probably because of this dream that Mordecai asks Esther to be silent about her origins. If God truly has a plan for her, if one day she becomes queen, which is how the dream can be interpreted, it is especially necessary that Ahasuerus not learn that she is a Jew. If he were to know that, he would not choose her for his wife, and the opportunity of salvation—this is some dream!—would disappear.

However, as important as they are, these dialogues, the one between the interior and the exterior of the palace and the one Mordecai carries on in the depths of his being, are not enough. It is still necessary that this communication be expressed through the people themselves. It is still necessary that it pass from nonverbal dialogue to audible dialogue. However this collaboration between men and women, between female and male works out, it just might be confrontational.

REBELLION AND DIPLOMACY

While Esther is being confronted with the harsh reality of harem life, its patriarchal laws, and the weighty and detestable responsibility of being queen, Mordecai is certainly experiencing her absence in a big way. Esther is closed up in the palace and inaccessible to him. They find themselves in diametrically opposite worlds. The life of a queen is not one that Jewish residents of Susa are familiar with, to say the least. Even Mordecai who enjoys certain privileges is remote from anything like that. Another difference however, more existential than this, is the difference between a man and a woman. Inscribed in their very being, their difference in sex implies different behaviors. We can imagine them like two very different cultures, but of equal value. In a patriarchal society, where an asymmetrical relationship between women and men is set up, this reality often goes unrecognized.

In order for this difference in behavior to be able to play a constructive role, it must not only be recognized, but also accepted. For Esther and Mordecai this process of recognition and acceptance goes through a transformation from the experience of the physical absence of the other to a revelation of the depth of their being.

Mordecai, who is doubtless the head of the local Jewish assembly, becomes the head of an open rebellion outside the palace. Inside the palace Esther is playing the role of diplomat. Her fine intelligence, her knowledge of the customs, as well as her relative caution allow her to remain in contact with Haman as well as with her own people and so avoid the catastrophe of a rupture.

Two ways of behaving amount to two tactics which, when they enter into dialogue, will let a solution to the conflict between Mordecai and Haman be found. However, in order for that to become possible, Mordecai has to renounce his power over Esther. He must accept giving up the initiative and letting her act freely as seems best to her and be free to be herself. This is the price he has to pay in order to discover his own true self.

Then a strategy of dialogue between the inside and the outside, between rebellion and diplomacy, develops (2:11, 19, 21). Non-verbal dialogue gives way to real communication, which becomes possible thanks to a eunuch whose confidence Esther has won. Mordecai can now inform her of the plot against Ahasuerus, and she in turn can unveil its existence to the king (2:22–23).

MAN AND WOMAN AS COUNTERPARTS

Chapter 4 of the book of Esther is a good illustration of the constant comings and goings between the outside and the inside of the palace, and also an illustration of the back and forth between a man and a woman. It also shows how two strategies, reflections of two cultures complement each other instead of being exclusive. Mordecai ends up falling in with Esther's arguments. He accepts the idea of a fast by the people, which the queen and her servants join (4:16–17). Alongside this nonviolent and general rebellion, Esther continues with her own strategy. As we have seen, she organizes banquets, a very feminine tactic which will end up with the fall of Haman and the salvation of the Jews.

In the end this way of life in dialogue, where the difference between acting like a woman and acting like a man is fundamentally respected, bursts into full solidarity when Haman's plan is disclosed. The still relatively hidden dialogue can become open communication. Esther and Mordecai encounter no further obstacle to working together. Man and woman are henceforth publicly face-to-face partners engaged in a symmetrical relationship.

Amidst all the imponderables of the story, Esther always found a way to put into practice her vocation as a partner, sometimes with a man, sometimes against a man. She is the image of the woman, in the full meaning of the word (cf. Gen 2:18–23). When it was essential, Esther dared to be against Mordecai without ceasing to be with him. Her unfailing solidarity is the best confirmation he can expect in terms of his dream. It is also thanks to her that his situation is radically transformed. From being prey for the gallows, he becomes a personage whose influence will be as great outside as inside the palace (8:7–15; 9:4). Nothing any longer happens in the court of Ahasuerus without the influence of either Esther or Mordecai.

Thus because they could keep alive in themselves their particular vision of history, because they dared to obey their deep intuition and respect the otherness and the difference in each other, because they continued in dialogue as a couple although not without pain, Esther and Mordecai realized their full vocation as human beings. A man and a woman in partnership, equal yet different, united yet separate, God found them to be just the partners necessary to shield the Jews of Persia from hatred and save them from extermination.

Conclusion
Journey to the End of Exile

THE TIME OF EXILE allowed the Jews of Mesopotamia to engage in a conversation with another culture. This was possible because Cyrus had inaugurated a policy of cultural toleration. Persian civilization became a source of enrichment as it stimulated and fertilized Jewish thought. After all, it was from the time of exile that the Jews brought back Aramaic which would become their national language. It is also at this time that they began to use the Babylonian calendar and to consider days as beginning the evening before.

PILGRIMS OF FAITH

If we find evidence of adaptation to the surrounding culture in the book of Esther, we also find awareness that the process is full of risks, that there are limits that must not be crossed. In confrontation with a totalitarian power, the cult of personality, and anti-Semitism, Esther and Mordecai refuse to compromise. They choose the way of civil and religious disobedience. They deal with impending catastrophes courageously. They insist on being faithful to their Jewish identity when faced with a power that seeks to deny their origins. Instead of assimilation, they prefer a culture of difference. Instead of the Babylonian gods, they prefer their God. Even when their God is momentarily hidden and silent, their God is nonetheless the giver of their Torah.

This obedience to their deep identity, to God's plan for his people, to a story that starts before they were born and will last way beyond their lifetimes, this obedient faithfulness to what is essential permits Esther and Mordecai to complete their perilous journey to the end of exile. And we see that it is by this kind of women and men that history is made and that totalitarianism is overcome. When death and extermination had all but occurred, life bursts forth to the amazement of the nations and the Jews alike.

In the book of Esther deportation and exile are from the outset of course lived as a geographical reality. But these are so much more than that. They are also a cultural and religious reality. The delicate balance between respect for the civil, social, and political laws of the Persian Empire and at the same time fidelity to their spiritual calling permit the deportees to discover the inner dimension of exile, an experience they begin to see as constitutive of human life itself.

Abraham and Sarah were the first aliens to wander between countries, from one culture to another. The Jews of Susa are in this way joining the spiritual family whose members are always in one way or another strangers and sojourners on earth. In the Bible a journey often comes with a double meaning. On the one hand it is a change of geography and on the other it is a spiritual adventure. When God asks Abraham and Sarah to leave their country for another (Gen 12:1), it is not simply a matter of leaving their homes and families. As Rashi says, this departure is also an inner movement, a journey "for their own benefit as they explore their inner being." It is a matter of becoming who we are called to be for God and for others. The traveler, the alien, is transformed into a pilgrim of faith.

A STEP ON AN INNER JOURNEY

So it is that onto the deportees' long march to Babylon is superimposed the beginning of a long journey into themselves. We have observed how Esther and Mordecai had to use all their moral and creative strength in order to preserve their Jewish identity. If we in turn want to take our place among the descendants of Abraham and Sarah, we will have to undergo a similar form of exile because this is what undergirds the ethical search, the fulfillment of God's plan for the human race.

So with Esther as our guide perhaps we can be led to the discovery that this sort of "self in exile" is ultimately the shortest path to living in our deepest self, the place where God abides. It is a paradoxical adventure that transforms exile into communion and that has in store for us the surprise of encouraging self-knowledge to emerge just as we discover God's mercy. This seems to be the experience of "Esther's three days."

In our day there are many people who are living in this kind of a time of testing. Men, women, children, old people have the sad experience of wandering in the hope of finding a place where they might re-embark on a life worthy of the name. Can we welcome them as members of the family of Abraham and Sarah? For others exile assumes the form of unemployment, divorce, separation, marginality. The fragility of all human relations is of course one of the characteristics of our age.

Still others experience exile in their religious lives, and this takes many forms too. Some no longer find their church a place where they can live out their faith, so they join new spiritual movements or sects. But others, like Esther and Mordecai, undertake a courageous confrontation. Conscious of the gravity of their situation, but also of the opportunity of the moment, they devise new ways of remaining faithful. Base communities, house churches, liberation movements, and new theologies, all testify to how exile can bear fruit when it is lived as spiritual nomadism rooted in Scripture.

ANTI-SEMITISM YESTERDAY AND TODAY

The book of Esther reflects, as in a mirror it seems, so many aspects of our own time. Manifestations of racism and anti-Semitism, as well as nationalism on all sides, show that we have not yet rooted out of our society that modern Amalek that was Hitler. In the face of this sad statement of fact the book of Esther, while it brings no definite solution to the struggle against evil, can nevertheless keep us awake, make us vigilant. It is with this vigilance that we can see the anti-Semitic and racist arguments of all times in the arguments presented to Ahasuerus by his chief official. "There is a certain people scattered and separated among the peoples in all the provinces of your kingdom; their laws are different from those of every other people, and they do not keep the king's laws, so that it is not appropriate for the king to tolerate them" (Esth 3:8).

But anti-Semitism does not arise from the Jewish condition itself. In reality it is the projection onto the Jew, into the Jew, of the image of the Jew we make for ourselves. Anti-Semitism plays a revealing role in the history of the nations. It is the measure of the degree of humanity in a society, ethnic group, or nation. Throughout history the Jew has been thought of as a stranger and a foreigner, as strangeness itself. The Jew incarnates in his real-life experience the human condition as we find it in the Bible—a stranger and sojourner in the land. For those of us whose way of life is more or less sedentary this fundamental fact about the human being is little by little getting lost. We so easily forget or prefer to ignore the bond of kinship that unites us to the stranger. Do we not all have the same need to be understood, welcomed, loved, accepted, and recognized?

Alongside its revealing role, anti-Semitism is in its secular dimension an open door to all the forms of racism in history. And anti-Semitism, in its religious dimension as the rejection of Judaism, is an open door to all the divisions that exist among the three families that claim to be followers of Abraham. The book of Esther therefore puts a double challenge before us—the challenge of our relationship to the stranger and that of our encounter with the Jew.

In our societies of abundance the stranger reminds us of our own fragility, of our limits. This is perhaps what makes us unconsciously fearful. In the presence of this danger, either we deport or isolate the stranger, or we demand that he assimilate and renounce his sense of identity. But we can get over our fear of the stranger and instead see her as an opportunity instead. The opportunity is to recognize that our personal and collective richness is made up of our diversity. The other, whether an individual or a society, is precious to us in the measure by which he differs from us. The stranger represents for our age a unique opportunity to develop true toleration in our midst, a real "culture of difference" in fact. As for the challenge that the encounter with Judaism represents for Christianity, we can envisage it in the form of a dialogue of differences which, far from being mutually exclusive, can be mutually enriching.

A SPIRITUALITY OF DIFFERENCE

In order to renew the broken bonds of two thousand years, we must dare to make overtures to each other. In these days of interfaith dialogue and much interfaith misunderstanding at the same time it is, in my opinion, more necessary than ever before to take our lead from Paul and recognize that the church is a branch of the synagogue tree (Rom 11). Both communities, with the challenges for each to the success of this task, have to open themselves to this dialogue. In real ways the future of a huge sector of the human community depends on it.

Personally, I believe that we must never fear losing our Christian identity in recognizing that Jesus is fully Jewish. It is time to bring to an end an exile that has lasted far too long. We must give him back his roots and at the same time recover our own. Then we will no longer fear being inspired by Jewish tradition since it is the tradition of Jesus of Nazareth.

I remain convinced that without an ongoing dialogue with Judaism our Christian life and our theology will continue to be menaced with impoverishment, confusion, substitution, and ultimately rejection. The Shoah, which has been called "Christianity's failure," tragically reminds of this. Being oblivious to the chosen people soon turns into sidelining them, which little by little degenerates into hatred, into anti-Semitism. Therefore this incredible, but alas historical, paradox arises—the church of the Jew Jesus and of the Jew Mary challenges its own roots and dishonors itself when it denies them. For the Church is only a graft on the tree that bears it (Rom 11:12–29).

The book of Esther therefore poses the incontrovertible question of the existence of the other. This is the issue of otherness and difference, and also the issue of peace or war. Will we have the courage to answer it in the manner of Esther and Mordecai, knowing how to distinguish practical compromise from compromise of principles, and remain faithful to our identity, our roots, our history? Is this not the only way we can discover our differences to be a source of enrichment and develop not only a culture but also a spirituality of difference?

Bibliography

Bolens, Lucie. *La Bible et l'histoire au féminin*. Geneva: Métropolis, 1982.

Laurencin, Marie. "Le Calmant." In *Le Carnet des nuits*, Geneva: Pierre Cailler, 1956.

Wiesel, Elie. *Paroles d'étranger*. Paris: Le Seuil, 1982.

The Zohar: Pritzker Edition. Translated by Daniel C. Matt. Stanford, CA: Stanford University Press, 2004.